The events and characters in this book are entirely fictitious.

Nothing like this has ever actually happened.

TABLE OF CONTENTS

I. It's not Marketing if People Want It

II. Must be Able to Juggle Priorities

III. A Topical Chapter on AI

IV. Can I Just Scan Your Badge?

V. The Client Wants a Face to Face

VI. The Appraisal

VII. The Senior Hire

VIII. Using Your Initiative

IX. The Corporate Response

X. Not every Event has a GTM Tag

CHAPTER I

It's not Marketing if people want it

If you want to work in marketing, or just can't think of anything else to do, try to find someone who will pay you to market something people already want.

Jenny was the Marketing Manager for a tech company that sold software that nobody could live without to other tech companies that sold software that nobody could live without.

At her interview, the CEO told Jenny that everybody who heard about the product loved it. They just needed more people to hear about it. Slick Inc had tried everything already. They just needed someone new to try harder.

Jenny's main job was to post things on LinkedIn to help people understand that they couldn't live without at least a bit more software.

The job was much more difficult than it sounds. Because of carousels. And because some buyers were Millenials but some were Gen X that hadn't died yet.

Jenny had just passed her six month probabtion and the company only had another 18 months to fire her for no reason at all. Like the last seven Marketing Managers.

Half the problem in the world of marketing is unreasonable expectations and the other half is people not being up to the job.

Jenny decided not to have any expectations and work really hard. The CEO said she was a bright girl.

CHAPTER II
Must be able to juggle priorities

Jenny was in charge of lots of things. Not a budget, team or any agencies, though, because Slick Inc was lean.

The main things Jenny were in charge of were:

Making sure everyone had enough pens (because pens had the logo on and so were a marketing responsibility)

Replying to every email in the spam inbox, because the CEO said it showed "responsitivity" which was a word he learned on a leadership course.

Sending emails that would land in other people's spam inbox.

Any mistake in any document anyone in the company sent out, because Marketing should have checked it.

Achieveing a CPA of £900 without changing anything on the website, or doing email marketing, or using video, or changing any propositions, or evolving the visual identity so it didn't look like it was designed in Word in 2006 or broadening the paid ads platforms because "we tried those things and none of them worked".

Of the various reponsibilities, the last was by far the hardest, but the one everyone talked about least except for once a quarter when the chair of board would say, "still nothing happening on that CPA," and Jenny would wonder why he thought the CPA would change when nothing else ever did.

Jenny's favourite daydream was that the Chair of Board read the data analysis she shared with the CEO. But he was

too important and she too unimportant for that to be at all appropriate.

Everyone loved Jenny.

But no-one knew what Jenny did.

Sometimes would people say things like, "have you got a guillotine?" And when Jenny said she did not, they would say "Sorry. I thought you were Marketing."

Helen was the other woman who worked at Slick Inc. But she was a developer with AWS certification, so she didn't count.

Jenny's desk was in a corner under the stairs and sometimes people's coffee spilled on her head. But she was valued.

You see, over and over again, Jenny made it pretty.

Sales decks, release notes, board presentations, the boardroom, the communal kitchen, the website.

When the important work had been done either by men, or by women who didn't listen to Taylor Swift, Jenny made it pretty. Everyone thought she was brilliant at it, but Jenny felt a bit of a fraud as she was merely applying basic UX and CRO principles backed by various A/B test strategies.

A good career option in a world increasingly dominated by AI is to be good at things that everyone else thinks are beneath them but you can't get a robot to do yet. And smile.

By this, her seventh month, Jenny had acquired new responsibilities by popular consent:

Finding files in OneDrive and sending them to people

Everyone's email signature

YOU'VE BEEN HERE SIX MONTHS AND WE'RE STILL NOT SEEING YOU GET US ANY MORE LEADS THAN THE OLD MARKETING MANAGER.

NONE OF THIS IS HELPING ME WANT TO GIVE YOU A BUDGET OR ANY AUTONOMY, JENNY. YOU'VE GOT TO LOOK AT IT FROM MY PERSPECTVE.

THIS WHOLE MARKETING THING...IT'S JUST AN IDEA! IN ALL MY YEARS OF RUNNING A BUSINESS I'VE NEVER ACTUALLY SEEN IT WORK.

AND ANY SANE PERSON HAS GOT TO ASK WHY THAT IS.

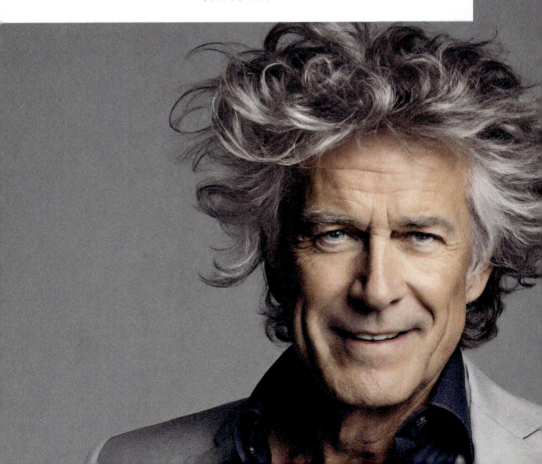

Sending everyone in the company logo at least 27 times a year without ever asking why. Then sending it again but BIGGER or BACKWARDS.

Backwards is what developers mean by reverse out. But if you call a cable a wire one time they will hunt you down and kill you. Whilst wearing T-shirts with cartoon characters on.

Nobody knew what had happened to all the marketing managers before Jenny. They just knew that they were all absolutely lovely girls, but not the right fit.

No-one could tell Jenny what any of these people had done, but they were quick to reassure her that, whatever it was, none of them were any good at it.

CHAPTER III

A topical chapter on AI

Since ChatGPT came along people had started questioning why they needed Jenny.

ChatGPT could do everything a marketer could do but faster, at a lower cost, and using great words like "delve" and "orchestration" without it expecting you to ask how its weekend was.

Jenny's colleagues hadn't realised that ChatGPT could write code too, and that writing code for computers was much easier than getting people to feel passionate enough about software to drop a million quid when Gartner said that 30 other softwares did the job better.

Jenny hoped they found out soon because the rollbacks after every new release were time consuming to message.

When it came to AI, Jenny was personally more interested in the automation of decision-making in the early vendor selection stage and the application of basic machine learning to purchased data combined with public data sets to identify accounts likely to be in market.

When Jenny did her MSc in Marketing, it was mainly about data.

The idea was you use a lot of actual data which you get out of actual software and do some graphs of it, and then you decide things and it's called being data-driven.

Everybody wants a marketer who's data-driven. Unless you show them data that their growth predictions are

incompatible with current market trends and their TAM is wildly optimistic. Then they just want you to run up some new creatives for Meta.

If you want a promotion then you take all the data and put it in a PowerPoint. Or you could use Canva, to show you were modern, and cheap. But always use the right fonts. When other people use the wrong fonts is is an oversight. But when a marketing person does it they're just being unprofessional really.

Jenny's boss was even cleverer than data. He had a gut feeling.

This helped Jenny to live in the real world not some marketing textbook.

Jenny's boss said that the things Jenny posted on social media were too long.

People hate reading! He would tell her.

The CEO said, that his daughter said, that Jenny could do a lot worse than post a photo of a cat on LinkedIn. The CEO sent her a PNG of his cat on WhatsApp.

It was the same sort of cat that Taylor Swift had. If Jenny photoshopped a branded baseball cap on it, It would be called Marketing or possibly even a meme (which is the best Marketing of all).

Jenny asked some of the developers what they thought about the idea, and they all agreed: the CEO was always right.

So Jenny posted the cat. No-one liked it but Jenny's boss was happy. Jenny decided not to overthink this.

Sometimes Jenny had small misunderstandings with her colleagues.

A lot of these misunderstandings came about because Jenny talked in made up words or marketing bullshit that nobody understood but Jenny.

And the rest of them came about because Jenny didn't understand normal concepts such as data layers and the differences betweent a J-SON connector and an API.

Jenny was all wrong. But everybody was terribly kind about it. They loved her ENERGY.

CHAPTER IV
Can I just scan your badge?

The biggest thing Jenny managed was events.

After sales had decided which event to go to Jenny would book the stand, design the stand, get the stand printed, wheel the stand to the exhibition, and put the stand up.

She also booked the train tickets for the sales team, because it made sense if one person did it, even though they all lived in different cities.

At the show, Jenny could see that everyone knew she was on it as they would be keen to draw on her expertise, asking questions like: "What time is lunch?", "Was it this quiet last year?" and "Have you got a pen?"

The CEO thought events were an expensive waste of time. People should click on ads and fill in a lead form, he said. When there were no leads, he said this proved he was right. And when there were leads he'd say they weren't real leads. And when they were real leads, he congratulated the sales team.

Jenny tried to explain about multi-channel campaigning and how investment in events supported paid advertising and the risks of allowing competitors to dominate the personal connection opportunities provided. The CEO said, "I went to a show in 2009 and we spent £60k and do you do how many sales we got? Not a single one."

Jenny's undergraduate degree was in molecular biology and she graduated with a first. But thinking about that is just an example of Millenial entitlement.

The CEO left school at 16 and it had never held him back.

At night, Jenny made earrings out of clay and sold them on her UK Etsy site, which she'd integrated to her personal socials and promoted through PPC and a structured SEO process whilst being fully GDPR compliant and deploying a first-party data system.

At weekends Jenny took her earrings and bracelets and necklaces to craft fairs, where she had a QR code letting customers sign up to her email newsletter for discounts and to join her loyalty scheme.

Jenny didn't post about her earrings on LinkedIn because if anyone realised that Jenny was a real person who cared about things, she would lose all respect at work.

Plus, as her boss said, earrings isn't a real business.

Earrings don't have recurring revenue.

People found Jenny very old fashioned for writing things down. After all, it was a tech company, and Jenny should know better than anyone that writing things down wasn't "on brand".

Everyone else remembered things without writing them down. They used Fireflies.Ai to tkae all their notes and send them to their inbox where they could delete them, and anyway Jenny typed up notes from all the meetings and sent them to the whole team.

Writing things down was probably what Jenny was most famous for, so far. "Look out," people would say, "She's got her notebook!"

Banter meant people liked you. Jenny had to remind herself that men show respect through belittlement and not to be oversensitive.

CHAPTER V

The client wants to meet F2F and everyone loses their shit

One November, Slick Inc's biggest customer decided to visit all the way from a big city in the US which we can't name even though none of this ever happened, actually.

The software wasn't working as they expected and this was a problem because they were a very important company and also because they had expected the software to work and also because they'd only signed a one-year deal and so couldn't be fobbed off without it impacting on revenue targets.

Support had logged all the tickets but dev hadn't picked them up. They were already working on the backlog AND the

roadmap. Support should really have explained to the customer that they shouldn't expect complex technology to work all the time but they hadn't bothered.

Another problem was that Neil, who was the only person who knew how the software worked, had left in September because he found having to come into the office one day a week "oppressive".

Now that the Visual Identity Evolve had been put on hold because "changing the colours isn't going to fix the CPA," Jenny found she had less and less to do. Everything was with the CEO but "everything" involved making changes and as the CEO said, "anyone can have an idea. I've got ideas. What we need is results!"

Jenny stayed productive by watering the plants. And when the milk ran out, she would walk to the shop and buy more.

Teamwork was important at Slick Inc and so often her colleagues would help her out by saying, "Jenny we're out of milk."

Jenny was in charge of these things because plants and hot drinks are ultimately about how people feel. And that's what marketing was. Absolutely nothing that happened at Slick Inc was about gender stereotypes. After all the CEO's wife was a woman, which proved he couldn't be sexist.

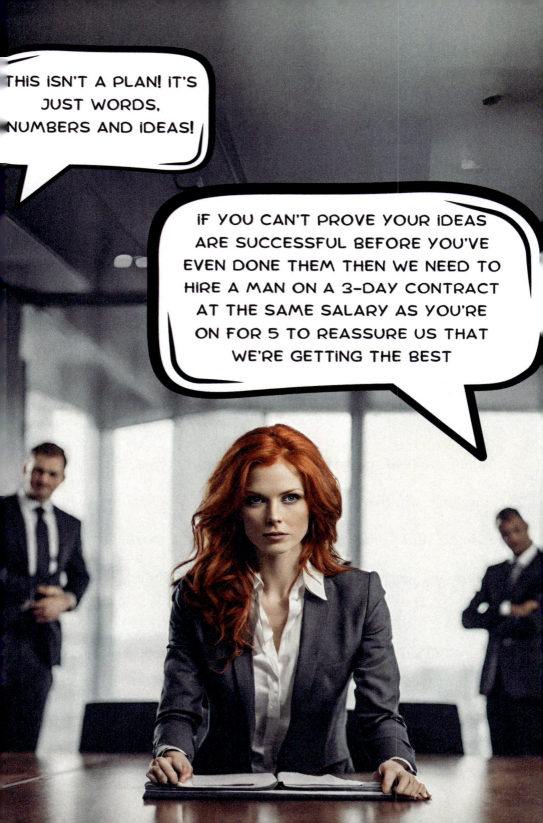

The week before the visitors came Jenny filled the fruit bowls, and bought new mugs with the company logo on in case the visitors forgot where we they were or tried to steal the crockery.

She painted the office by staying late every evening because Jenny wearing jeans and climbing ladders in office hours was only going to distract the devs. The CEO said he was surprised she hadn't thought of it herself given she claimed to care about marketing so much.

When the visitors arrived, Jenny brought coffee and doughnuts to the board room once an hour. On Tuesday a woman said, "what do you think Jenny as a marketer about what Google are likely to do with privacy sandbox?"

The CEO said, "Don't talk to Jenny about sandboxes! Jenny thinks a sandbox is something you find in a playground!"

Everybody laughed. Jenny made sure to keep on laughing after everyone else had stopped. So she didn't cry.

Jenny re-sent the email she'd written to the CEO three weeks ago with the list of areas across the business in which they were in breach of various international data privacy laws with her suggestions for compliance management and reporting.

At the top of the email she put "Sorry to chase you!" so the CEO didn't think that Jenny thought he should ever have to reply to an email if he didn't feel like it.

The CEO replied straight away. He said, "We need a table for 15 tonight at Vecchia Nonna."

Vecchia Nonna were full but eventually she got a table for 9pm when she shared her personal social accounts and promised to do a free review vid for them at the weekend.

Jenny didn't have a corporate card. "Why do you need a card? You're never going to go anywhere or meet anyone." the CEO explained.

So she booked it on her personal card because using your initiative was important and because the CEO liked people to come to him with solutions, not with problems.

Jenny turned up at Vecchia Nonna at nine. The client team included a number of global marketing specialists it would be good to learn from. Plus she could post a photo of it on LinkedIn.

But when she went to sit at the table the CEO asked for a word.

He said the dinner would be very boring for Jenny as they'd be talking about APIs and all sorts of things Jenny wasn't interested in. He said she should wait in a cafe ready to book everyone Ubers when they were ready to leave.

Jenny called her Mum when she waited. Jenny's Mum had never worked in business but she did used to watch Ally McBeal in the 1990s so she knew the score. Her Mum said, "The problem with you is you're a complete doormat. People will treat you the way you let them treat you."

Jenny wasn't adopted. But she often wished she could be.

CHAPTER VI
The Appraisal

It was time for Jenny's annual appraisal, which was conducted through software because that's the best way to do everything really.

Everyone pretended that the annual appraisal was about strengths and weakensses but really it was about how much more money they'd give you.

Jenny was a woman so she knew that the best way to get more money was never to tell anyone that you wanted more money but to hope for it secretly and be nice.

HOW HAS YOUR LINE MANAGER ENABLED YOUR SUCCESS IN THE LAST 12 MONTHS?

HOW DO YOU PLAN TO CONTRIBUTE TO OUR GROWTH BY DOING 'MORE WITH LESS' NEXT YEAR?

WHAT PERSONAL FAILINGS HAVE LED TO YOUR KPIS NOT BEING DELIVERED?

HOW HAVE YOU GONE 'ABOVE AND BEYOND WHAT IS HUMANLY POSSIBLE' IN THE LAST 12 MONTHS?

THINKING ABOUT THE NEXT FIVE YEARS, HOW SMALL OF A PAY RISE WOULD IT TAKE YOU TO RETAIN YOU (REMEMBER WE OFFER A 5% COPMANY DISCOUNT ON A POPULAR SANDWICH CHAIN?)

GROWING THROUGH PEOPLE TOGETHER

Anyway some things were more important than money.

Like being able to change your job title on LinkedIn from Marketing Manager to Head of Marketing, and having all the other department leads realise that she was as valued as they were and they shouldn't ask her to fetch their sandwiches.

The more Jenny thought about it, the more convinced she became that if only she had the title Head of Marketing, all the other problems would go away.

Jenny was working on her need for external validation. At the same time, what she really needed before she'd be ready to deal with her issues, was more external validation.

The CEO had to cancel Jenny's appraisal in the end because his daughter had grazed her knee playing lacrosse at her posh private school and he had to get to the school first because he was divorcing his wife and wanted to make a point.

He sent her an email with some bullets:

- Hugely valued team player
- Needs to work on her communication
- Needs to work on her understanding of technology
- Less emails please
- Don't let data become a distraction to getting the job done
- CPA

At the bottom of the email he put:

Can you enter all this into the HR system please. Great work. Keep it up!

CHAPTER VII

The senior hire

A week later the CEO told Jenny he was hiring a VP of marketing.

"I need someone with more clout," he said.

"Someone who's going to be more strategic. Someone who's going to be able to work with James and Mark and Phil and Ben and Steve and Nick and Josh and Seb. Someone whose going to understand the tech. And not just post cats on social media and buy donuts.

"Though thank you for all your hard work on those things. But you know really get into the data side of things. All that stuff you hate."

Someone you can really learn from. This will be great for you. John starts on Monday. Can you get him set up on the system and make sure you order a corporate credit card for him. Everybody loves you Jenny. And can you check your emails please? I need you to make the annual report look pretty. Put some graphs in, you know."

Jenny drove home the long way. She stopped at the wine shop.

Why was she so angry? Something was wrong with her. She was angry all the time!

Mark wasn't angry and Steve wasn't angry and Ben and James and Nick and Seb. No-one seemed angry except for her.

Everyone else was happy being paid much more than Jenny and not having to go into the office so much because

"marketing is about collaboration". Every fucking one else was absolutely fine.

Jenny was the problem. Probably, Jenny had been a problem her entire life. Everyone hated Jenny and her fake Marketing shit and her jpegs.

Jenny had learned how to code in Python and R on her MSc. It didn't stop the Head of Dev telling her there was no point in explaining new features to her because she wouldn't understand.

And every time Jenny offered to run an NLP analysis of customer and competitor reviews to identify new service and product and messaging innovations, or to use a simple ML exercise to predict churn using number of calls to support, engagement with socials, email CTR and platform usage, she was told:

That sounds quite ambitious. Why don't we just work off some basic assumptions?

Jenny thought of all the support and encouragement she had had at Slick Inc. She was "enthusiastic, passionate, helpful, energetic". She'd had so much praise for things that didn't count, she'd not noticed what was missing.

Jenny thought, actually, there was something else. Something that no-one had ever said to her at Slick Inc: Jenny was smart.

And it was exhausting pretending not to be.

Maybe what else was exhausting was, making everyone look better at their jobs than they were.

Somewhere she'd agreed to a deal that was a very bad bargain: say yes to everything asked of her and take the blame when it didn't work.

CHAPTER VIII

Using Your initiative

When Jenny got home, she had a message on Insta.

Hey Jenny our podcast guest for this week has had to pull out and I wondered if we could do a record with you? Love your earrings and what you've done with your shop. You are Queen of the Side Hustle and that's what we're about...what do you say?

Jenny had always wanted to be on a podcast so she could post about being on a podcast on LinkedIn.

But the rules were clear. The mass layoffs in Big Tech had panicked a bunch of previously meek employees to start all kinds of side hustles. Using their own time to make money of

which the company got no share. Slick Inc's lawyers had moved quickly to ban any employee working for anyone else or being a director of any company, even their own.

The CEO tolerated Jenny's earrings business but had made it clear, "there's a clear conflict of interests. Since we are trusting you to manage marketing for us as an enterprise-focused security software company, you selling clay earrings on Etsy, or even having a personal social media account really, is bound to raise questions about your loyalty.

"I'll turn a blind eye for now but we'd be quite within our rights to dismiss you for this. As your contract clearly states, all your energy and creativity should be directed towards achieving revenue targets for Slick Inc."

So Jenny messaged the podcaster back and said, "no thanks."

Next, a Slack notification flashed up. It was from the Head of Dev.

"Hey Jenny. These release notes need to go out tonight. Can you make sure they go out before 10pm because we're going live in three AWS zones then. CEO has confirmed you are OK to do this. Just make them pretty before you send! P.S. These are the notes you were chasing me for last week but it's obviously very busy in dev right now."

Two ideas struck Jenny: the first was, that if she didn't do this, the company would look really bad to its customers.

The second was, that she no longer cared.

Jenny opened the bottle of wine that she was given as a Christmas Gift by the CEO. She took a deep breath, put her phone on flight mode and...

Jenny installed a cookie banner on the website. Now they could resume Google Ads in the face of Consent Mode 2 as well as demonstrate the same legislative compliance their clients were used to working to.

Jenny logged into the notetaking app that logs all CS calls and replaced the testimonials the CEO had written for the website with real customer comments. They were credible, real, varied and relatable.

Jenny changed "thousands of customers" to "major global customers". It's more credible given their specialism.

Jenny deleted the features on the website that they hadn't built yet and which she personally thought were the major

contributor to a paltry 13% close rate for sales and a churn rate twice that of industry average.

Jenny opens a second bottle of wine.

She forwarded the email from the Head of Dev to the entire customer base and copied him in.

She posted on the company Linkedin account with a video of her dancing in her kitchen to "Upgrade U" by Beyonce featuring Jay-Z and writes a caption which said:

"If the Social Media Manager will go to these lengths to get you to consider upgrading your security infrastructure, just imagine how hard the rest of the team will work to deliver your project on time and budget."

CHAPTER IX
The Corporate Response

The CEO acted decisively.

He called John. The new VP of Marketing.

John said he'd seen it before. Jenny was probably realising that a lot of errors were going to come to light and expectations were going to rise. Having an MSc in marketing was all very well, but if she was so good, why was she so cheap? Also Millenials just couldn't handle stress.

He said Jenny had too many opinions and she tried to hijack conversations with data. If she'd been that good, why didn't her last company fight to keep her? Best to end her now.

The CEO phoned the recruitment agency and asked them to

"IF YOU CAN'T COPE WITH BEING TOLD WHAT TO DO WITHOUT HAVING THE RESOURCES TO DO IT WHILST LIVING IN THE NEAR CERTAINTY THAT THE PLANET WILL DESTRUCT BY THE TIME YOU'RE IN EARLY OLD AGE AND ROBOTS WILL TAKE YOUR JOB IN FIVE YEARS WHILST HELPING YOUR PARENTS SYNC THEIR APPLE DEVICES ACROSS THEIR FIRST AND SECOND HOMES WHILST BEING GASLIT ANYTHING HAS CHANGED IN TERMS OF ACCEPTANCE OF DIVERSITY AND AS THE UK'S INFRASTRUCTURE COLLAPSES TO A LEVEL BENEATH THAT OF ITS FORMER COLONIES, THEN, AND I'M SORRY, BUT YOU'RE NOT CUT OUT FOR SAAS."

find a new marketing manager. He agreed to pay them 20% more than Jenny had been on. But if they asked for 30% they could have it.

He sent an email advising all staff that Jenny had personal issues to work through and that anyone who cared about her should in no account contact her or like any of her LinkedIn posts, for Jenny's sake.

He waited three hours and sent a second email announcing that overnight two massive leads had come in as web enquiries and he needed everyone to pull together to make sure they closed.

"There's no such thing as Marketing. It's all just luck, isn't it. Serendipity that we try and graph because we don't understand it at all," he reflected poetically as he asked the company accountant to retrospectively change the pension contract so he could pay off his ex-wife.

CHAPTER X

Not every event has a GTM tag

Jenny fell into a near-suicidal state of depression and anxiety which her friends supported her through by texting her every few days asking, "Have you got a new job yet?"

She went to the doctor and got put on medication. The doctor saw a lot of marketers and said actually he thought that the pressure to prove attribution for social organic wasn't helping global mental health.

Jenny applied for 276 new jobs but the feedback was always the same: if you don't like your job the best thing to do is stay in it, but do minimal work, so that you look in-demand and reliable.

Jenny kept applying for jobs and told herself: next time she'd be stronger. She'd not take things personally. She'd not be so arrogant as to expect her ideas to carry sway. She was only 35 and really you shouldn't expect anyone to listen to you until you're at least 40. Then you've got a good eight years as a woman til they think you're past it.

People who criticize everything you do only do it because they care. They only do it because their standards are higher than yours. If you criticize yourself in your own head enough, then there's no room left for them to hurt you more.

Sometimes she thought about focusing on her earring business but the things she used to love seemed to pain her now. She read Instagram posts telling her to believe in herself. She called the Samaritans until they asked her to stop.

After a few months Jenny saw that John the Senior Hire had

left Slick Inc.

Then she saw someone called Jane had been brought in as Marketing Manager. On LinkedIn Jane said, she was excited at the huge opportunities to apply basic marketing principles to a company that was already 10 years old.

This Jane did a video of the CEO's cat, with the CEO's new girlfriend and used captions to relate it to cybersecurity in international banking. It was decent work.

Eventually Jenny got a final interview. She presented her 90-day plan. They loved it. They said they needed someone with fresh ideas and energy, just like her.

They offered her the job on the spot and Jenny accepted.

Jenny took at paycut but as the CEO said, she'd be making them so much money, he'd have to be an idiot not to give her

a rise.

Everything was going to be fine.

Jenny knew the phrase: if you fall off a horse, get back on.

No-one ever had told Jenny: if you fall off a horse, stay the hell away from horses.

No-one ever told her that camels, elephants and even tigers can also be ridden.

So Jenny got back on the horse that had only ever bitten and refused and thrown her.

Everything was going to be absolutely fine.

This CEO didn't have a cat.

AUTHOR BIO

Katherine Pomfret considers herself a marketer and has done since 1999 no matter what anybody else says.

You can follow her on linkedin.com/in/katherine-pomfret

for marketing insight

Or on twitter @indieretailgirl for jokes

Occasional cross-contamination does occur.

If you enjoyed this book, please write a view on Amazon.

Printed in Great Britain
by Amazon